My Yoga/My Way

Written and Illustrated by

Anne Cox

With reprint of I AM A YOGI - MY FIRST BOOK OF YOGA
and Spanish and French translations by Linda Alvarez

Archway Publishing books may be ordered through booksellers or by contacting:

Archway Publishing
1663 Liberty Drive
Bloomington, IN 47403
www.archwaypublishing.com
1 (888) 242-5904

Interior Graphics/Art Credit: Anne Cox
Photo Credits: Marisa Cox, Sandy Hall, and Doug Duncan

ISBN: 978-1-4808-8556-1 (sc)
ISBN: 978-1-4808-8555-4 (hc)
ISBN: 978-1-4808-8557-8 (e)

Print information available on the last page.

Archway Publishing rev. date: 02/19/2020

PREFACE

The purpose of my writing this book is to share some of what I know about yoga in a fun way. Yoga is not complicated because it's mostly about breathing, moving your body and then being still…. all with awareness. My hope is that you will use this book as a workbook for your own notes, drawings and ideas to do yoga YOUR WAY.

INTRODUCTION

Yoga is a lifestyle. It can be practiced for a lifetime… so start early. Remember to listen to your body and only do what you can do carefully and easily.

I wrote this book in first person with the intention of having the reader take possession of the practice presented on the pages and of the book itself. Poses are briefly described in text, and are meant to be copied from the image on the opposite page.

Play and have fun with Yoga Your Way.

Anne Cox

DEDICATION

I dedicate this book to all children of all ages and to parents and teachers who wish to use it as a guide.

While learning through routine and self discipline, controlling breath, holding poses and self-calming, children will become confident in their abilities and self worth.

By developing core strength I believe they will find within themselves their own uniqueness and gifts and they will do it their way.

TABLE OF CONTENTS

BREATHING (PRANA)

BUMBLE BEE BREATH

I hear the buzz of bumble bees as I close my mouth, cover my eyes and put my thumbs over my ears and hum.

FEATHER BREATHING

Holding a fluffy feather a few inches from my nose,
see it flutter as I exhale through my mouth or nose.
I am aware of my breath, and I can control it.

ALTERNATE NOSTRIL BREATHING

I close one side of my nose and breathe through the other side 5 times. Then I repeat on the other side. I am clearing the passageways in my nostrils.

UJJAYI BREATH

Darth Vader and the Ocean

"What do Darth Vader and the ocean have in common?" asked Pops as he sat in the half-lotus position across from his grandson.

"I don't know, but I think I'm about to find out," answered Nick, while rolling out his bright orange mat on the bamboo floor of his grandfather's yoga studio.

In one smooth movement, he sat cross-legged facing his grandfather, their eyes connecting.

"I'll give you a big hint," offered Pops. "It's one of our five senses, but it's not sight, touch, smell or taste.

"That just leaves sound," said Nick.

"Right," laughed Pops. "In yoga, that sound is called **ujjayi** breath. It's pronounced **oo-ji**, and in Sanskrit, one of the ancient languages of India, it means breath with sound, or ocean breath. "Here, let me show you."

"Open your mouth and breathe slowly in and out, two times. Do you feel the air moving in the back of your throat?" Pops inquired.

Nodding his head, yes, Nick breathed, slowly, with his mouth open.

"Good, Now, close your mouth, but continue making the husky noise as air passes in and out of your nose," continued Pops.

In and out, in and out, slowly, Nick felt the warmth of his breath and he began to hear the raspy Darth Vader sound at the back of his throat. It was also the sound of the waves as he remembered walking on the ocean beach.

After a few concentrated breaths in the quiet setting of dim lights, mustard-colored walls and vases of fresh herbs from the garden, Nick whispered, "This is just a *'yoga thing'*, right Pops? Snoring on purpose?"

Pops answered, "It is basic to the practice of yoga. When we inhale, or breathe in, we take air into our lungs and that sustains and fuels our life. When we exhale, or breathe out, we are ridding our bodies of toxins, which cause illness and disease. When we learn to control our breathing, we can make ourselves feel better and feel confident. So it isn't *just a 'yoga thing,' it's a life thing."*

"It sounds like a lot of good can come from just knowing how to do **ujjayi** breathing," offered Nick.

"Absolutely! This is a skill, just like throwing a curve ball. In fact it would even improve throwing a curve ball," continued

Pops. "As we control our breathing, we can move more easily in everything we do. **Ujjayi** breathing clears our lungs and warms and calms us and gives us strength too."

"What about soccer?" said Nick. "Could **ujjayi** breathing help me play my favorite sport better?"

"Let's see if it would. As we meditate for a few minutes, you can picture how your new breath can improve your game," said Pops.

Nick imagined himself setting the soccer ball up for a pass to Justin…**ujjayi** breathe…kick! Perfect! Justin passed it back to him as he moved into position on the left side of the goal…**ujjayi** breathe…cross-kick into the goal for a score! That's control!

Nick blinked his eyes wide open. "I really felt in charge of that ball and I can't wait to try it in real life!"

Nick scrunched up his face and said, "Let's see if I remember how to do **ujjayi** breath. First, I open my mouth slightly and breathe slowly. Then I close my mouth and continue making the noise at the back of my throat as the air goes in and out of my nose. Got it!."

"What a wise grandson I have," said Pops, as he rolled up

his yoga mat and stacked it in the corner. He watched Nick rise off his mat and follow suit.

"That's your yoga lesson for today and I look forward to hearing about all the times and places you will remember to use **ujjayi** breath." Pops grinned. "See you at today's game, champ."

"See you, I love you Pops. And thanks!" Nick called back over his shoulder as he flew through the door. He was suddenly anxious to try out his new breathing technique, while thinking, *this is going to be a great game!*

LABYRINTH

Choose two colored pencils. Use one color to follow the Labryinth, beginning at the opening at the bottom of the page.

V-e-r-y s-l-o-w-l-y find your way to the toys in the middle. Then use the other color and from the center, re-trace your way back out. This is a fun way to meditate.

POSES (ASANA)

1/2 BUTTERFLY STRETCH

I stretch one leg out and fold the other one in. Then I lean my body over my outstretched leg and count to 5 or 10 and I repeat on my other side.

GARLAND BALANCE

Squatting with my knees apart, I place my arms between them.

My hands come together and I count to 5 or 10.

BRIDGE STRETCH & CORE

On my back, I lift my hips off the mat and hold bridge pose while I count to 5 or 10.

Draw your own fun yoga pose on this page.

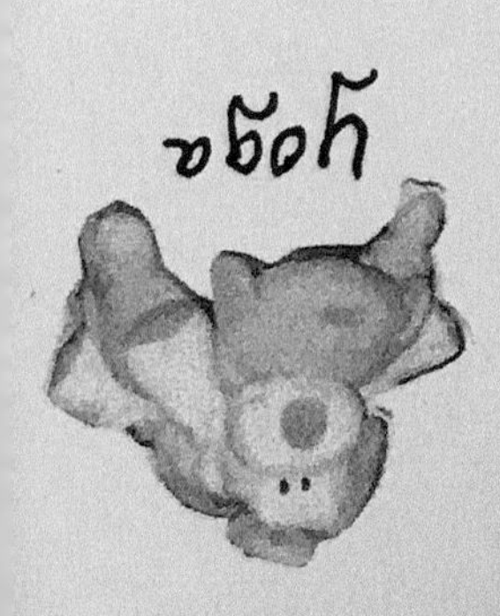

Make some notes you want to remember about yoga.

TREE POSE BALANCE

Standing on one leg, I bend my other one and place my foot above or below my knee. My arms reach up like tree branches. I repeat with my other leg.

Note:

(Begin learning this pose while near a wall. Without leaning on it, you can touch the wall with one finger)

CHAIR POSE CORE BALANCE

I bend as though I am going to sit in an imaginary chair and lean forward to balance with my arms out straight or on my knees. I count to 5 or 10.

BOAT CORE BALANCE

I balance on my bottom while lifting my legs up and then my arms. I hold boat pose to the count of about 5 or 10.

WARRIOR I

STRENGTH / BALANCE / CORE

I am strong with one leg forward and bent and my other leg reaching straight behind. I balance with my hands together and arms straight up. Then I repeat on my other side. I hold this pose and breathe from my belly as I count to 5 or 10.

WARRIOR II

STRENGTH / BALANCE / CORE

From Warrior I pose, I turn my upper body to the side and stretch my arms straight out, over my legs. Then I repeat on my other side. I hold this pose on each side as I count to 5 or 10.

FORWARD FOLD STRETCH

Bending my knees slightly, I fold my body forward, letting my head and arms relax as I count to 5 or 10. Then I slowly rise up as I continue to breathe.

LEGS UP INVERSION

On my back, I lift my legs straight up while my arms stay on the floor as I count to 5 or 10.

CALMING (MEDITATION)

SAVASANA

CALM / REST / MEDITATION

I lie on my back, close my eyes and rest after my yoga practice. I just think about breathing.

Yea! Another Labyrinth!

I can strengthen all the main muscles in my body:

THE FIVE TIBETAN RITES

RITE 1 CIRCLES

I stretch my arms out and turn to the right 3 turns.

RITE 2 VICTORY V

I lie on floor and lift my legs and head together, repeating the movement 3 times.

RITE 3 CAMEL

On my knees, (arms down to my sides) I lift my shoulders, sliding my hands along my hips and tilt my head back. Sliding back to beginning position, I repeat the movements 3 times.

TIBETAN 4 OPEN/CLOSE TABLE

I sit on the floor with my legs straight out. Pushing up to hands and feet I am in open table. Sliding back down to sitting, I am in closed table. I repeat the movements 3 times.

RITE 5 ACTIVE DOG

Starting out on my belly, I press up to upward facing dog. Pushing back and up, I am in downward facing dog. I repeat the movements 3 times.

I USE MY YOGA BOOKS MY WAY

I Am a Yogi—
My First Book of Yoga
Written and Illustrated by
ANNE COX

I sit on my mat with
my legs crossed.
This is called

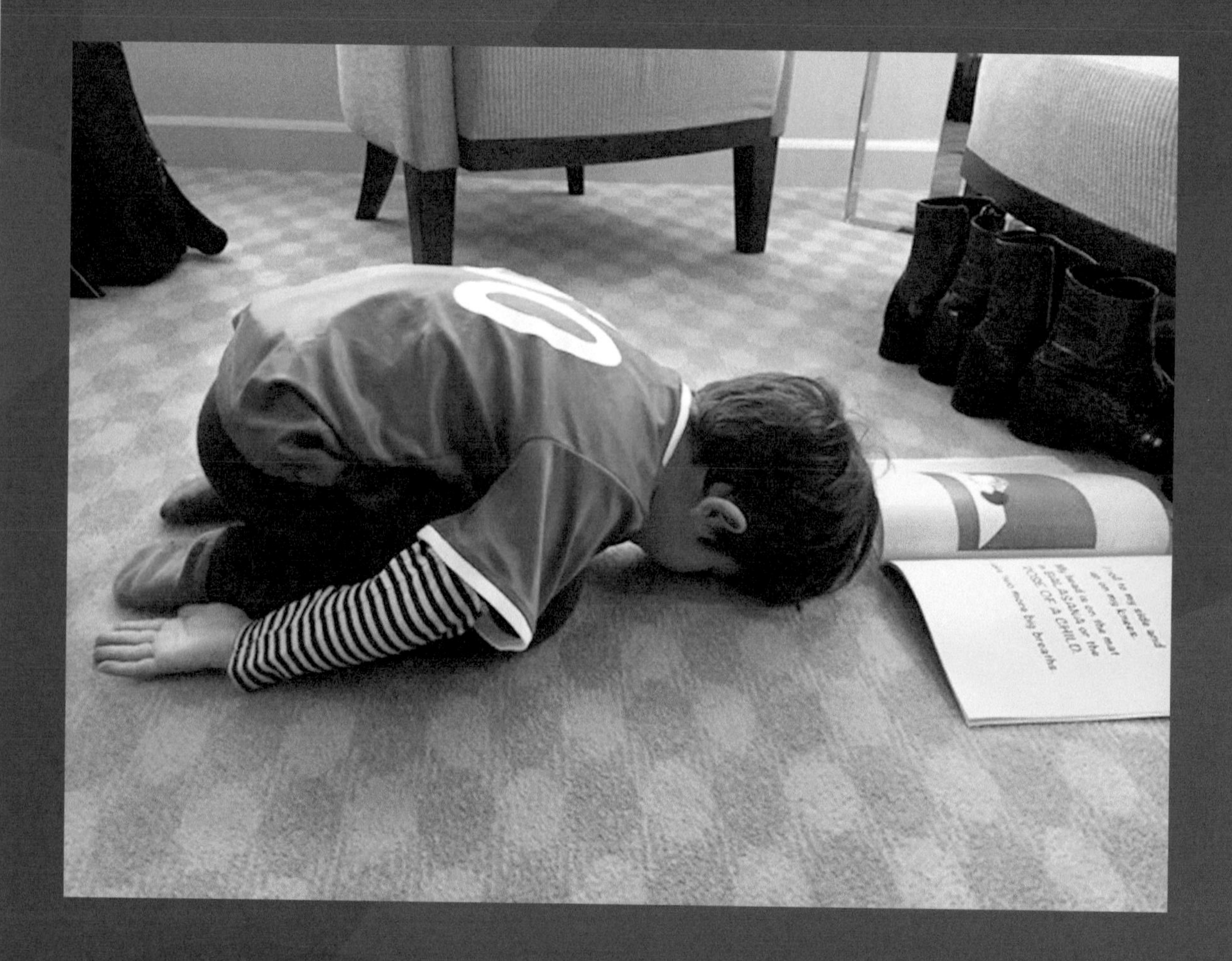

to my side and
on my knees.
head is on the mat
BALASANA or the
OF A CHILD.
more big breaths.

I Am a Yogi—

My First Book of Yoga

Written and illustrated by

ANNE COX

This is my yoga mat. I roll
it out on the floor.

Esta es mi estera de yoga. La
desenrollo sobre el piso.

Ceci est mon tapis de yoga.
Je le déroule sur le sol.

I sit on my mat with my
legs crossed. This is called
SUKASANA or EASY POSE.

Me siento sobre mi estera con
las piernas cruzadas. Esta
postura se llama SUKASANA
o POSICION SEDENTE.

Je m' assois sur le tapis avec
mes jambes croisées. C' est
la posture SUKASANA ou
LA POSTURE FACILE.

I reach my arms up to
gather my energy.

Levanto los brasos con las palmas
juntas para concentrar mi energia.

Je lève les bras en haut pour
recueillir mon énergie.

I bring my hands to my heart
and take two big breaths.

Con las manos cerca del corazón
respiro profundamente dos veces.

Je ramène mes mains vers
mon coeur et prend deux
grandes respirations.

I come to my knees and
hands for table pose.

Me pongo sobre las manos y
rodillas para la postura la mesa.

Avec les genoux et les mains sur le
tapis, je fais la posture de la table.

I puff out my tummy and take a big breath through my nose.

Me expando la barriguita y aspiro profundamente por la nariz.

Je gonfle mon ventre et je respire á fond par le nez.

Then I arch my back like a scary cat and blow out all the air.

Luego arqueo la espalda como un gato aterrado y espiro todo el aire.

Puis j´ arque mon dos comme un chat effrayant, et j´ expire tout mon air.

With my hands on the mat, I push up to my tiptoes and stretch my bottom to the sky. This is downward facing dog pose.

Con las manos sobre la estera me levanto a los dedos de los pies y levanto las caderas hacia el cielo. Esta es la postura el perro con el hocico hacia abajo.

Avec les mains sur le tapis, je me pousse sur la pointe des pieds et je m'étire les fesses vers le ciel. C' est la posture le chien museau vers le sol.

I lift my leg up to the sky, wag it like a dog's tail and bring it back to the floor. Then I do the other leg.

Me levanto la pierna hacia el cielo, la meneo como la cola de un perro, y la devuelvo al piso. Luego repito con la otra pierna.

Je lève ma jambe vers le ciel, je la remue comme la queue d'un chien et je la ramène sur le tapis. Puis je fais la meme chose avec l'autre jambe.

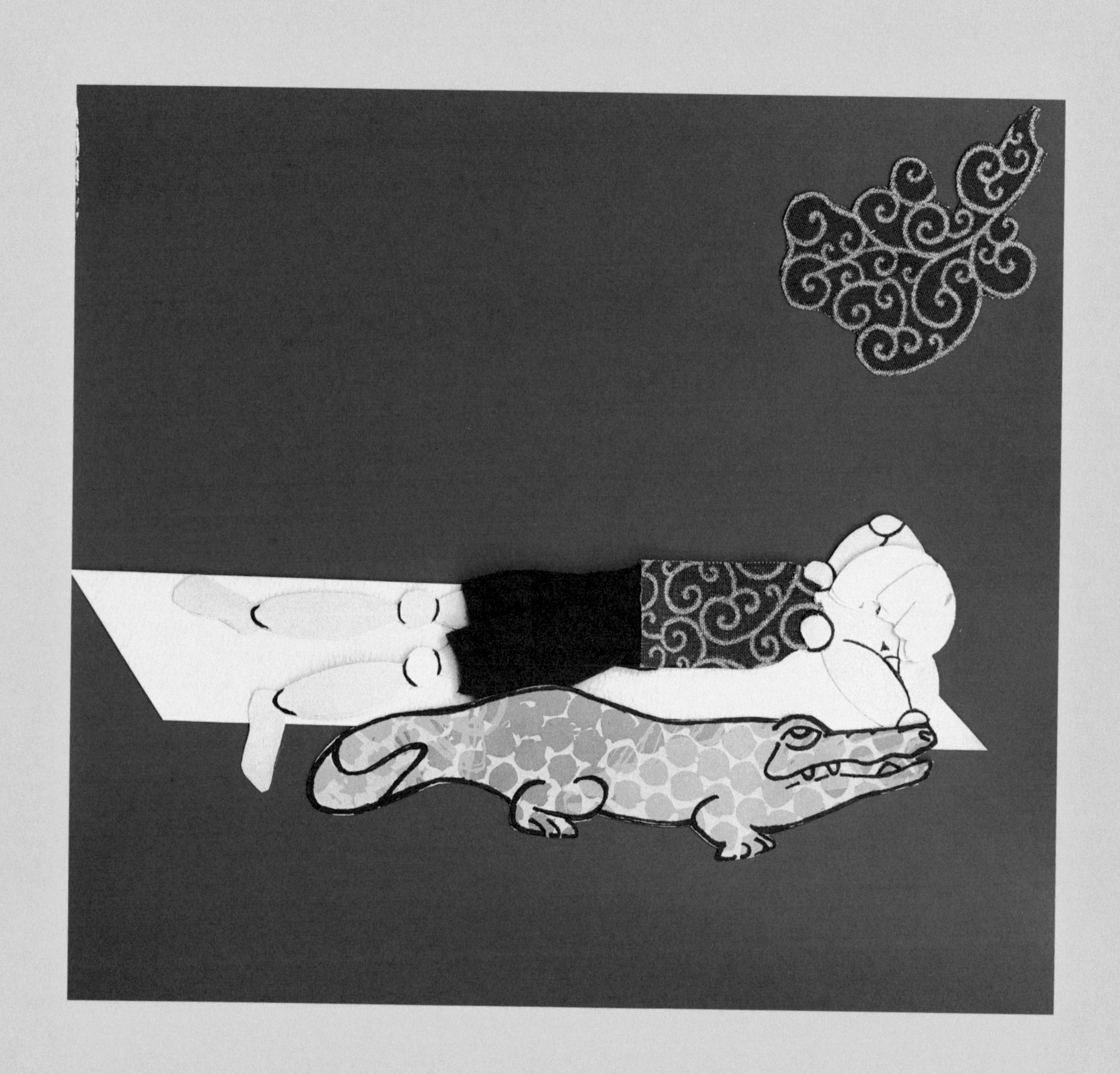

Now, I lie down on my tummy and
fold my arms under my head. My feet
turn out and I rest, breathing in and
out like a big green crocodile.

Ahora me acuesto boca abajo y doblo
los brazos debajo de la cabeza. Los
pies quedan abiertos y me descanso
respirando como un gran cocodrilo verde.

Maintenant, je m'allonge sur mon ventre
et je plie mes bras sous ma tête. Mes
pieds tournés vers l' extérieur, je me
repose. J'inspire et j'expire calmement
comme un gros crocodile vert.

I roll to my back. I bend my knees and hold my feet with my hands and rock side to side. I am in happy baby pose.

Volteo sobre mi espalda. Doblo las rodillas y sostengo las pies con las manos y me balanceo suavamente lado a lado. Estoy en la postura el niño feliz.

Je roule sur mon dos. Je fléchisse mes genoux et je tiens mes pieds avec mes mains, et me balance d'un coté à l'autre. Je suis dans la posture l'enfant content.

I roll to my side and up on my knees. My head is on the mat in balasana or pose of a child. I take two more big breaths.

Me ruedo a mi lado y me levanto a las rodillas. Mi cabeza esta sobre la estera en balasana o la postura el niño. Respiro profundamente dos veces.

Je roule sur le coté et me met sur les genoux. La tête est sur le tapis en balasana, ou la posture d' un enfant. Je prend deux grandes respirations.

I reach my arms up to the sky. I gather my energy and put my hands together. I bring them to my heart and say "NAMASTE."

Extiendo los brazos hacia el cielo concentrando mi energía. Luego pongo las palmas juntas cerca del corazon, y digo "NAMASTE."

Je léve mes bras vers le ciel. Je recueille mon énergie et je joins mes mains, une paume contre l'autre. Je ramène mes mains vers mon coeur, et je dis, "NAMASTE."

Namaste is used as a sign of seeing goodness in `self´ and in others. It means "bow me you" in Sanskrit, an ancient language of India.

Se usa la palabra "Namaste" como una señal para que tu puedas ver lo bueno en ti mismo y en otras personas. Namaste significa "me prostro a ti´ en Sanskrit, un idioma antiguo de la India.

Namaste c´est le mot utiliser pour indiquer qu´on voir la bonté de soi meme et des autres. Namaste veut dire "je vous salue de la tete." C´est un mot en Sanskrit, une langue très ancienne de l´Inde.

MANDALA

Mandala means circle, reminding us of our relationship to the world beyond and within our bodies and minds.

Color the mandala as you meditate on the shapes within the circle.

ACKNOWLEDGMENTS

I wish to thank Kilian for his playful approach to the practice of yoga and for inspiring the theme for this book and its cover. And to Waylon and Cecilia, I am grateful that they too, indulged their grandmother by posing so gracefully. Nick and Justin graciously critiqued the Ujjayi story and I made them the characters in it. Surprise!

Granddaughter Belle and a friend showed how to use their copies of my first yoga book and are perfect examples of how it works.

The second printing of "I Am a Yogi - My First Book of Yoga" allows me to introduce a new audience to yoga with translations into Spanish and French, by my dear multi-lingual friend Linda Alvarez, reviewed by Maud Jurez. I am hoping that with all three languages on each page, it will also expose every reader to two other languages; another way to have fun with yoga `your way´.

Doug and Linda Duncan graciously provided flora and fauna, as well as Doug's photography from his many travels, for background for my asana collages.

I'm so glad that Marisa Cox and Sandy Hall are handy with their cameras and shared candid photos for this book. I thank my husband, Gary Allman for his valuable input as the book came together and my creative publishing team, Morgan, Andy and Christian for making it all happen. And I thank you, all the readers of this book for taking time out of your busy lives to DO YOGA YOUR WAY!

Namaste,
Anne

ABOUT THE AUTHOR

Photo by Josh Mitchell.

Anne Cox is an artist, writer and yoga teacher. She has lived in Japan, Kansas, Pennsylvania, and Missouri. She has traveled the world and now lives in Springfield, Missouri with her husband, Gary and sheepdog Sofie. She has earned a Bachelor's of Fine Arts degree, a diploma from the Institute of Children's Literature and a 500 Hour Certification from the Registered Yoga Alliance.

Printed in the United States
By Bookmasters